*May the wonder of angels
give you peace and hope*

To Mom
Thank you for taking
me into your heart as your
daughter.
From
I love you
Karen

On Angels' Wings

new seasons™

a division of Publications International, Ltd.

Louis Weber, CEO
Publications International, Ltd.
7373 North Cicero Avenue
Lincolnwood, Illinois 60712

Permission is never granted for commercial purposes.

Manufactured in China.

8 7 6 5 4 3 2 1

ISBN: 0-7853-3519-6

Angels give themselves fully,
for they have seen the face of love.

Life seems to run wild,
but God holds the reins and
angels tend the harness.

Heaven is the fluttering of angels' wings,

the uproar of celestial songs,

the clamor of love run loose.

What joyous music to our earthly ears!

Angels are all around us, as far as the heart can see.

It's a comforting thought to know that angels work and
move among us to make the most of the love we have.

There isn't a valley steep enough

that an angel can't carry you through.

When you live with
a heart of compassion
you have the heart of an angel.
When you fill your life
with deeds of compassion
you do the work of an angel.

When we believe in each other, we act as angels,

giving our confidence and the power of our faith.

It is no small thing to look into another's eyes,

straight and true, and to say with sincerity,

"I believe in you."

Sometimes just believing takes the greatest faith of all.

Angels find us not only when we need them most,

but when we simply need them.

Angels are the closest thing to heaven

that we carry with us every day.

Every visible thing in this world

is put in the charge of an angel.

SAINT AUGUSTINE

When you feel lost, pause and look closely around you.

Somewhere, somehow, an angel will be waiting

to help you home.

All our lives we walk among
heavenly beings, whether
we believe in heaven or not.
All our lives we are
surrounded by individuals
who spend their lives
invisibly cheering us on.

Angels help lead us out of our own darkness

and into their divine light.

All in the wild March morning I heard the angels call;

It was when the moon was setting, and the dark was over all;

The trees began to whisper, and the wind began to roll,

And in the wild March morning I heard them call my soul.

ALFRED, LORD TENNYSON

Ask an angel what he has
and he will say, "enough."
Ask an angel what he needs and
he will say, "nothing."
Ask an angel what he knows
and he will say, "only love."

Love finds us all, one way or another. Love gives us, everyone, a reason to live and to hope. Love wraps its wings around our weakness and carries us all the way home.

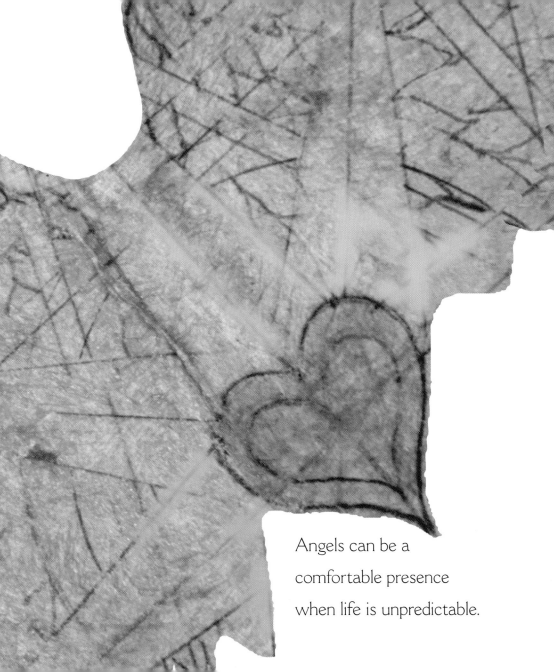

Angels can be a
comfortable presence
when life is unpredictable.

Happiness comes to those

who perceive the world

to be a loving place.

We do the best we can
and leave the rest
to the invisible souls
who walk beside us.

Make yourself familiar with the angels,

and behold them frequently in spirit

for without being seen,

they are present with you.

SAINT FRANCIS DeSALES

The days,

the hours,

the minutes of our lives

are guarded and observed

by angels.

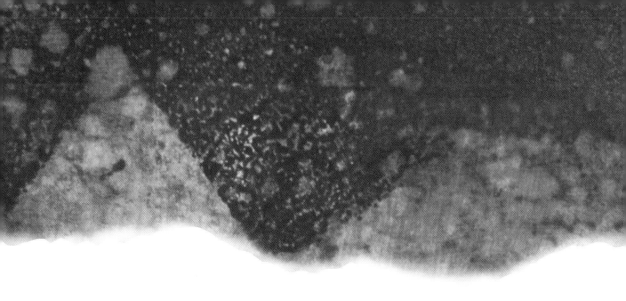

Riding on the wings of angels, you can see your life from a distance and

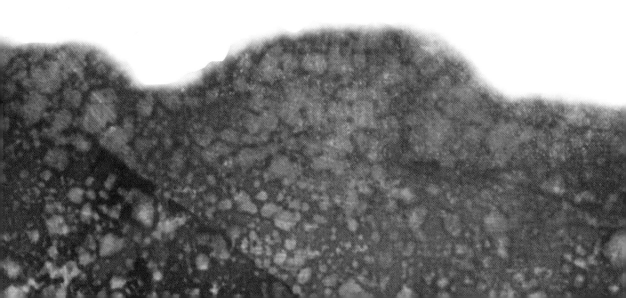

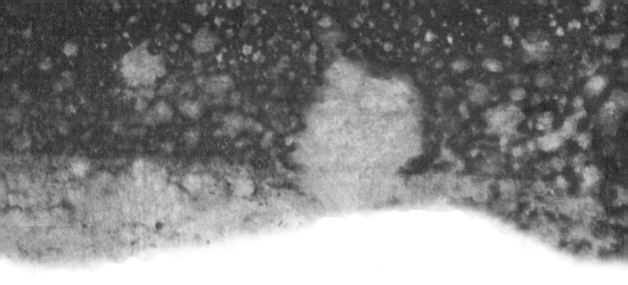

let go of the small and unimportant concerns that hold you down.

No matter the difficult people who cross
our paths, there is goodness in this world.
It is there because we are surrounded by
the goodness of angels and the goodness
they help us cultivate in ourselves.

When you feel the urge to **dance**, do it. When you find the will to **sing**, sing loudly.

When you catch a glimpse of glory, stand in **awe**. That is what angels do.

Through the eyes of faith we see the company we keep.

Angels have watched humans fight for freedom
since time began. Perhaps they wonder why we do
not celebrate, as well, the joy of belonging.

Hold on to your dreams; they will help
guide you on your own path to happiness.

. . . If honor be given
to princes and governors . . .
there is far more reason
for it being given to angels, in
whom the splendor
of the Divine glory is far more
abundantly displayed.

JOHN CALVIN

Angels meet us coming and going. They cross our paths. They walk by our sides. They lead us and follow us and rise above us and pave the ground beneath us. They do whatever it takes to help us do the things that God has called us to do.

Angels are everyday wonders. They are reminders to us that life is not just what we see and touch, or what we define and explain. Life is also invisible friends and protectors who stand by us to the end.

Angels can come to us in many ways, in many shapes and sizes, in laughter and tears, in happiness as well as sorrow. Angels are here with us in every part of life, helping us, loving us, helping us to love.

We do the work
of angels when
we reach out to
someone in need of
comfort or love.

Those who choose

    to see the good in people

        will be comforted

            by the goodness that abounds.

Surround yourself with the serenity of nature and
you will feel more at peace with yourself and your world.

Allow yourself
some time for
silence.

It will help to
regenerate
your spirit.

Most of the time life
whispers only soft clues,
gently suggesting the path to
follow. Heed the whispers.
Learn the language.
When you comprehend their
meaning, dreams can be
attained and hopes fulfilled.

The unlikeliest of
people harbor haloes
beneath their hats.

beyond ourselves

...eading our wings to fly.

Doris Jean Malloy

Doris Jean Malloy died Thursday, Oct. 31, 2002, at her home.

She was born Sept. 12, 1931, in Calhoun, Ky., and lived in Salinas for 38 years.

Memberships: Women's auxiliary of the American Legion Post No. 31, and the Women's Order of the Moose Lodge Post No. 658.

She was a fan of both Elvis and the Giants and enjoyed watching her grandchildren play sports.

Survivors: Children, Diane Malloy of Salinas, Douglas R. Vause of Sylvania, Ohio, Bradley C. Vause of Monterey and Ray W. Malloy of Cuyahoga Falls, Ohio; sisters, Yvonne Varner of Streetsboro, Ohio, and Charleen Medina of Akron, Ohio; brother, Richard D. Higgs of Ravenna, Ohio; and six grandchildren.

Services: 2 p.m. Wednesday, Nov. 6, at the Healey Mortuary Chapel, 405 N. Sanborn Road, Salinas.

Memorials: Make a Wish Foundation, 120 Montgomery St, Suite 1080, San Francisco 94104.

A wise person accepts the help she is offered.

A foolish person swears she'll do it herself.

A wise person shows gratitude.

A foolish person needs glory.

A wise person dances with the rhythm of her angels.

A foolish person trudges to nobody's drum.

To hope is to fly.

To fly is to dream.

To dream is to believe.

To believe is to do.

To do is to give hope.

To give hope is to do

the work of angels.

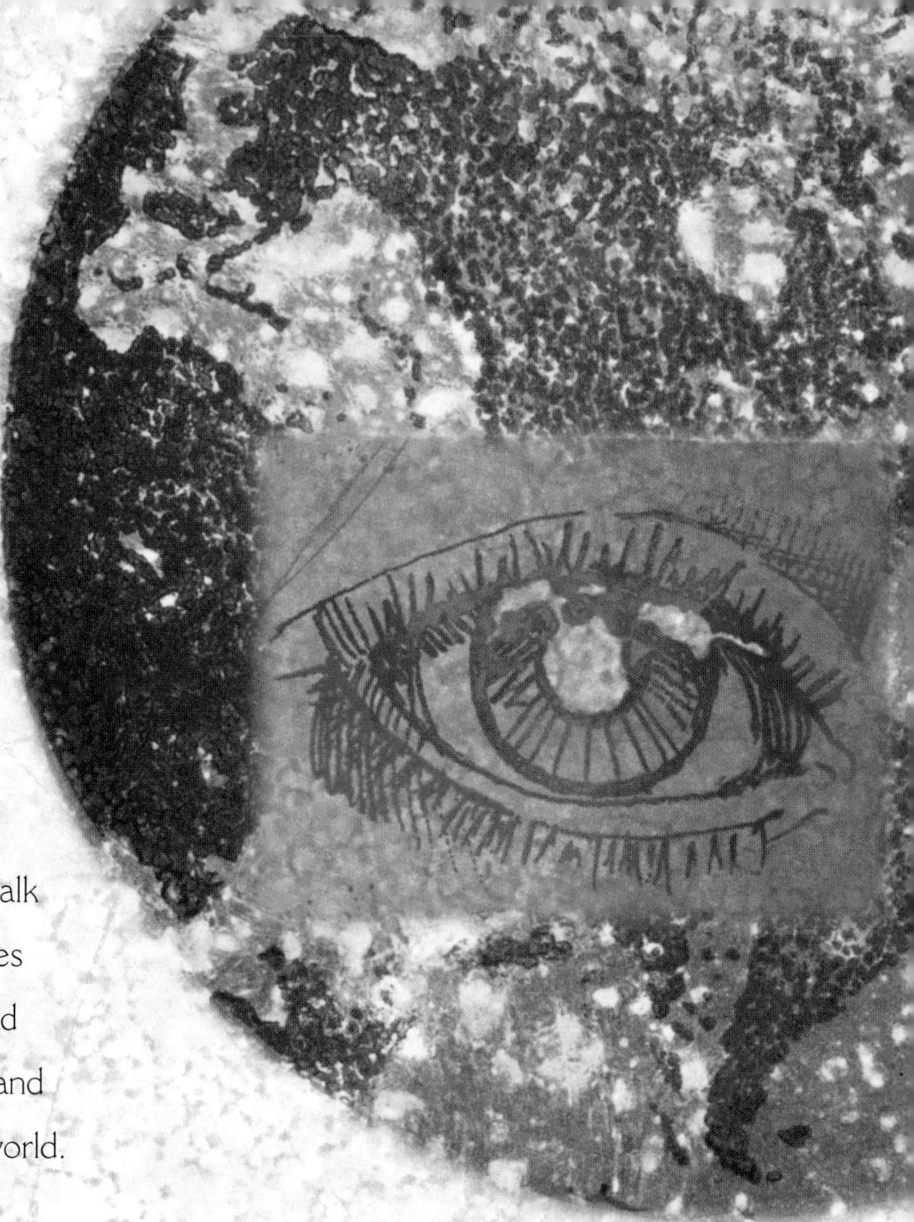

Those who walk
with their eyes
straight ahead
see all the joy and
wonder in the world.

Angels give their best
to help us do our best.

The road is winding that leads us home, but our angels are kind

and let us go as slowly as we need to in order to make the trip.

Do not forget to
entertain strangers,
for by so doing some
people have
entertained angels
without knowing it.

HEBREWS 13:2

A guardian angel o'er his life presiding,

doubling his pleasures, and his cares dividing.

SAMUEL ROGERS

Angels do the work of love:

love around us,

love within us,

love compelling us,

love igniting us.

We stand as tall as
angels when we kneel
to help a friend.

Keep your eyes on your own road.

That is the only one you have the power to change.

That is the only one your angels will be walking today.

Angels do not
change your mind,
they patiently wait
until you do.

Angels have visited humanity by streams
and in deserts,
by cradles and by graves,
by altars and by bedsides.

Angels have touched us at the holiest

and earthiest of places,

but they have seldom left us

the same way they found us.